Wild Light of the Heart

A Collection of Poetry
by Mallika McCarthy

Published by Buster Bodhi Press, LLC

All rights reserved. © 2024 Mallika McCarthy
ISBN: 9798305285727
Cover and book design by Mark Andrew James Terry
Photography and Illustrations by Mallika McCarthy
Photograph on Page 8 by Patrick Creaven
Available on Amazon.com, Barnes & Noble online, and most online book sellers

TABLE OF CONTENTS

5	**Dedication**
7	**Foreword**
9	**Introduction**
11	**Prologue**
13	Wild Light Of The Heart
14	Carousel
16	Step Close In
19	**Innocence, Childhood, Spring**
20	Trespassing
22	Changeling Child
23	Just One Peek
24	Delicate
27	Freefall
28	Shared Water
31	Mirror To The Sky
32	Motherline
34	No Corners
35	Lionhearted
35	Cracked Open
36	Apple Magic
37	Spring Evening
39	**Blossoming, Love, Summer**
40	Garlic
41	Roses
42	Meeting By The Lake
44	Good Things
46	I Love This Place
47	Imagine
48	Alchemy
49	Wheel Of Fortune
50	Light Within
51	Bear
53	Midsummer's Night
53	Remembered Kisses
54	Full Circle
56	Until Always

59	**Change, Loss, Death, Autumn**
61	Twilight
62	Lone Wolf
64	Held Hostage
66	A Heady Intimacy
67	Wash Me Clean
68	Demeter
69	Ashes Of The Morning
71	Trickster
72	When Death Comes Calling
74	Journey
75	Sanctuary
76	Slow Light
78	Watching The World From My Window
80	In The City Of Sand
83	**Wisdom, Grace, Renewal, Winter**
84	Threshold
85	A Storm With No Name
86	Sancta Maria
86	Stripped Away
87	First Frost
88	Old Spells
89	Winter Queen
90	The Longest Night
91	Grace
92	The Cailleach Tree
93	Quiver Shot
95	Sea Spray
96	Hope Kindles Hope
99	**Epilogue**
100	Unmapped Territory
101	Bright Horizon
103	P.S.
105	**Notes**
107	**Acknowledgements**
109	**Author's Biography**

Dedicated

to my true wolfpack, my wild-at-hearts

who run with me through the bright fields of forever

under ancient stars

FOREWORD

Meet Mallika - sage, poetess, mystic, wood nymph, faerie, songwriter, singer, yogini, dweller and caretaker of the ancient Irish myths and mysteries...I could go on but it's best you discover her for yourself.

Mallika will stir your sleeping embers.
She will make you cry simply by describing her morning walk...so be prepared. You are about to reach a deeper part of yourself, where tears of joy and longing flow like... well...like the river she strolls along in the evening twilight...

I have known Mallika since she was a child of five years old - the first time we met, she was wandering around in the sunny garden of the commune we both lived in, listening to her walkman (it was back then!).

I asked her if I could hear what she was listening to.

She handed me the headphones...maybe slightly miffed at being interrupted...but she did it anyway...and to my great joy, on the tape I heard the sound of ocean waves lapping on the shore and rolling in the distant depths. She was listening to the music of the sea... And that was when I first fell in love with Mallika.

Reconnected, forty years on, she suddenly sent me some of her poetry - and I knew I had the inevitable responsibility to share it with the world.

Enter Joe Cavanaugh and Mark Terry, two poetry aficionados, and fine poets themselves, who, like me, fell under her magic. Joe and Mark agreed with me, Mallika's poems had to be heard, and the rest, as they say, is history.

I am truly honoured to introduce you to such an extraordinary beautiful human being.

~ Miten

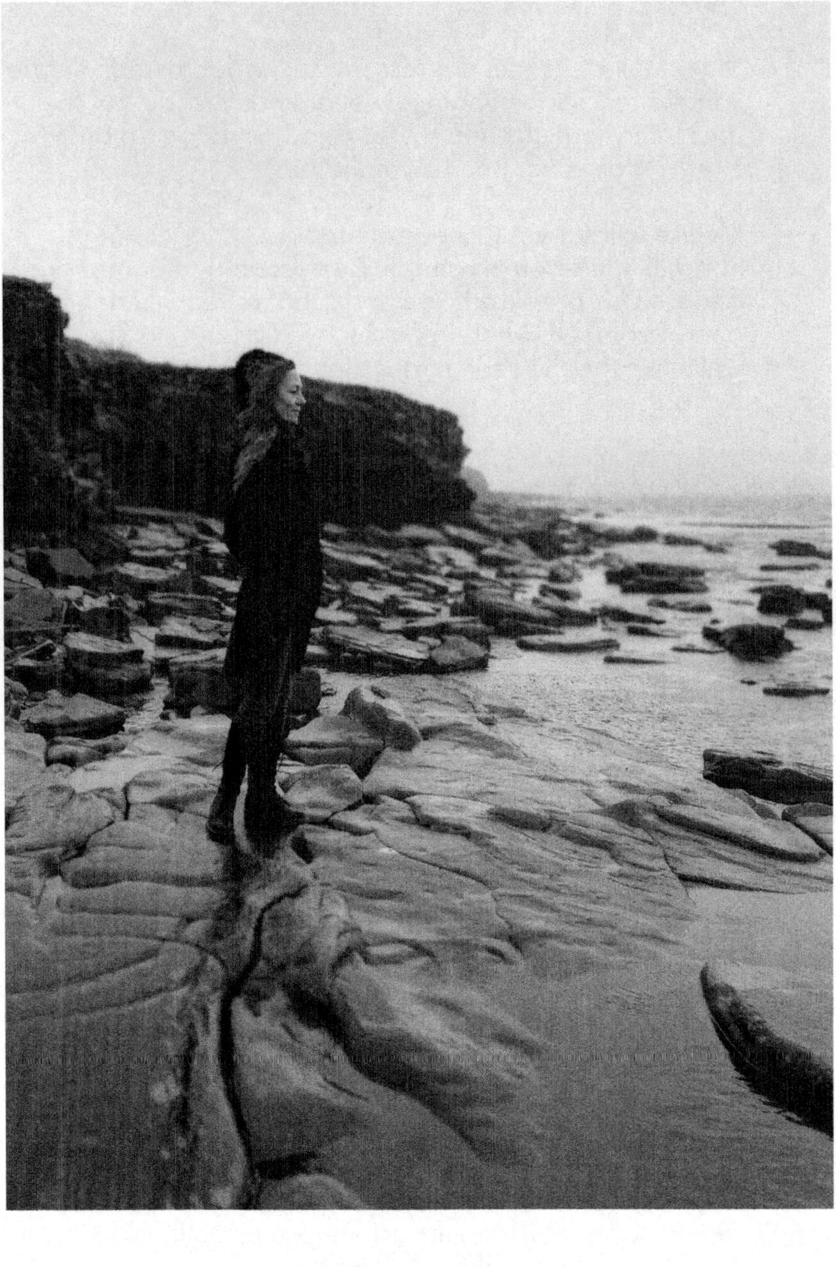

INTRODUCTION

This collection of poetry is born from the inner landscapes of my life, weaving the turbulent skies and vast oceans I live beside, into the cycles of love, loss and transformation that I have danced through in recent years.

Poems of deep personal experience set against the changing wheel of seasons on the west coast of Ireland, peppered with illustrations in pen and ink, drawn from the inspiration of this wild landscape.

The poems are housed in a story arc, a profound tale told in four chapters. This brings us through the seasons and cycles of life, correlating innocence and childhood with spring, blossoming love with summer, death and letting go with autumn, and eventually wisdom, grace and renewal with winter.

True to storytelling style, I have included a prologue and an epilogue to begin and end the tale in the proper fashion.

After a lifetime of writing for my invisible friends, I am happy to present you with my first published work, a collection of 60 poems – selected from several hundred written in the last few years – sculpted into a single tale; personal reflections on my colourful life, "cast," as it is here, "in the wild light of the heart."

With love,

Mallika

Prologue

♡

WILD LIGHT OF THE HEART

Cast in the wild light of the heart
The jagged landscapes
Of my life
Look very different
Brighter somehow,
Richer
Deeper

I see storm-grey oceans
Awash with colour
Their rhythms singing to me
Persistently
In quiet melodies
Of dark teal, azure
Aquamarine, silver

As the nonchalant summer dies
Now autumn skies take centre stage
Alight with cloudburst radiance
Wheeling rook-song
A festival act
For the changing days

The mountains' complex shadows
Inspiring me
To walk unsung paths again
In a cloak of muted feathers
Shot with brilliant blue
Carrying ink and pen
To capture their brooding beauty
With each step

* * *

CAROUSEL

This globe,
Like an ageing carousel
Spins in the darkness
Shadowed by vast galaxies

Ornate horses canter by
Glass-eyed
Fierce-browed
Manes tossed like wild waves
On a static sea

Paint peeling
Hooves prancing
They dance us through the seasons
Bringing us from winter into spring
Galloping fleet-footed
Through fields of daffodils
Past hedgerows
Bright with blackthorn blossom

And on through summer's long days
Along warm stone beaches
Out past midnight bonfires
Burning fierce under purple skies

See the wooden horses run
With loosened reins and
Tattered saddle cloths
In fraying red and gold brocade

Chomping bits
Through dawns they fly
Scattering the golden-brown leaves
Of autumn's finest rake-piles
With hollow wooden hooves
Striking muddied woodland paths
Like muffled drums
They run with snorted breath
And rolling eyes

Past squirrels gathering in their harvest
Bears lumbering to ancient caves
To sleep the snows away
Through glades of pines
Where no birds sing
For all have flown
To other springs
In warmer climes
Leaving the land to winter's slow decline

Oh still the horses ride
Running ever in circles
Turning the seasons' wheel
Powering day and night
Fuelling dreams with sparks of memory
Of painted horseshoes struck
On flint hillsides

So all eras come to pass,
While kingdoms fall and empires rise
Still the carousel it turns
Marking time
Creating brand new worlds

* * *

STEP CLOSE IN

Come now
Step close in
For love is like a diamond
Reflecting everything

Offer it up
Like sand to the sky
With both hands wide open
No matter how long we're given
This life is for living

* * *

Innocence, Childhood, Spring

TRESPASSING

When I was little
No barrier was sacred
Not even a locked door

But to be fair
How would anybody know
Not to cross a dry stone wall
If they'd never seen one before?

Healthy boundaries they call them
Keeps what's yours in and others out
Unless you give them permission
To climb your walls
Knock them down
Or leap the locked gates like a scout

They say the wind can blow through them
These lines drawn in stone
So the land can still breathe
You can keep what you own
And stone walls won't fall
Under enthusiastic feet
Or the wild winter wind's siege

"What's PROSECUTED?"
I ask my five-year-old friend
As we're scampering through the woods
On another man's land
Blackthorn twigs in our hair
Moss stains on our knees
Berry stains on our hands

"It's where they can shoot you on sight
If they catch you trespassing"
Says she matter-of-factly
"Oh," says I, "Sounds nasty…
Maybe we should go back"

"No don't worry," says she
Wise already at five
Walking on past the sign
As casual as you could get

"Even if we meet old Mr McGregor
With his gun and his hat
He'll have to give us a warning the first time
An' he hasn't caught us yet"

* * *

CHANGELING CHILD

Fascinated by wolves
Barn owls and shooting stars
From an early age
Yet scared of the dark

I'd lie in bed
In the big old house
Hiding from vampires
Listening for distant howls in the night

Did you know
You can't be seen from outside
When you're wrapped
In a tight cloak of light?

But secretly I waited
For a monster to come
Even with my cloak of protection
So diligently spun

Longing to be captured
Claimed, tamed
By the poignant darkness
That joins us

Taken by creatures of the night
To live amongst them;
A changeling child
Longing to belong to someone

JUST ONE PEEK

Hiding
Still as a statue
In behind
The old coats
In the box-room wardrobe

I hold my breath
To stop the dust
From going up my nose
The scent of Granny's mothballs
Making my eyes sting

I want to sneeze so badly
But I don't
For I won't let myself
Give in

Listening to the others
Whispering in the spare room
Tiptoeing across the wide bare boards
Of the landing
Giggling as she finds them
One by one

Curious as a cat
With a flicking tail
I imagine creeping to the door
Taking just one peek
To see is she still looking

But I know I won't
So I steady my breath
To make sure I don't give in
For this time
I am determined to win

* * *

DELICATE

Bold as a child
I was a brave, brash
Bare-footed
Big-mouthed
Tree-climbing
Horse-wrangling
Storytelling
Cartwheeling
Wild one

My mother used to say
Treat yourself gently
The way you throw yourself through life
You're more delicate than you think
My little flower

But I wouldn't heed her
Nor would I take it from her
Sure, what would she know?

She was never around
She had no right
Too busy following her path
While I was left to find my own
And so I did

Now she's nine years gone
I'm starting to see
She had a unique perspective

After carrying me
Giving birth to me
Watching me grow as a child
Always looking in from the outside
From the other side of the world

Perhaps she was the one person
Who could really see me
Perhaps she was right
About the gentle flowering

For now
After decades
My delicate self
Is coming into the light

* * *

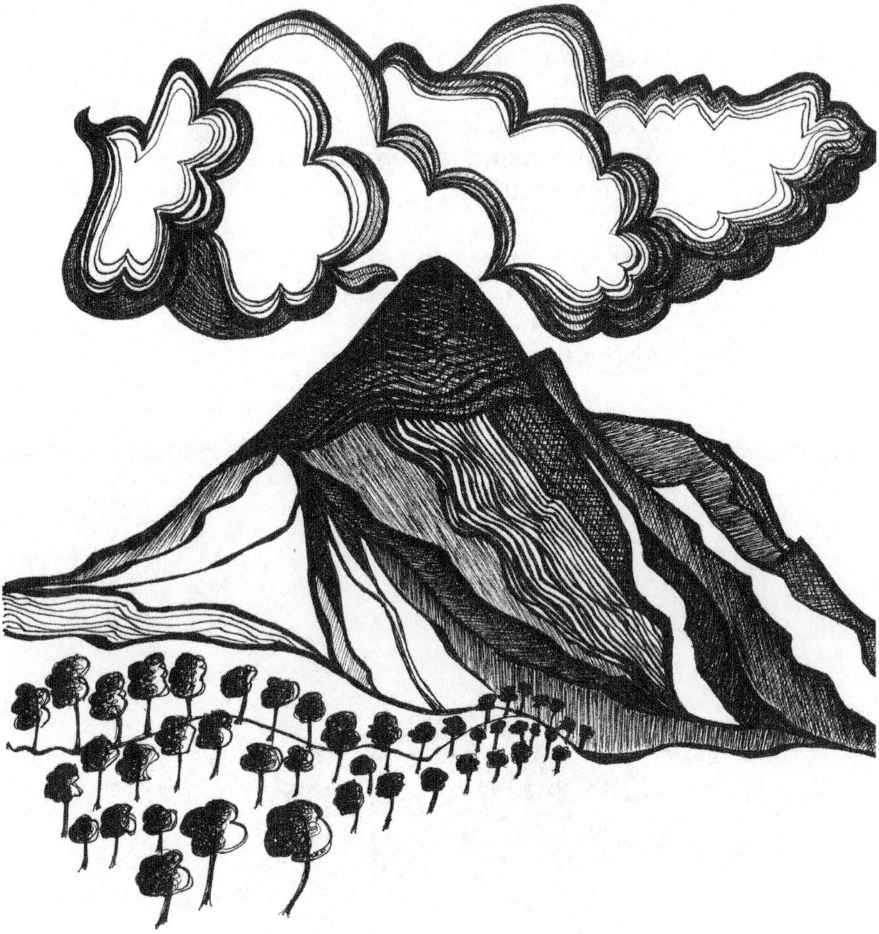

FREEFALL

There were rivers rushing
Down the road
that night

I remember the woods
in our borrowed car
Sliding sideways in the rain
on a winding track
As we flew through the trees
Skidding into freefall
Far above the valley

I remember
Looking for your glasses
in the wet, wet leaves
On the side of a hill in the dark
with no moonlight
"Can you see them, little Eke
Can you see?"

In the morning
you told me
As we watched them winch it
from the steep cliffside
How the car was only held
by one young tree
Slender as the circle of your fingers
Filled with running sap
That let it flex and bend
without breaking

Linked by winter streams
rushing through mountain valleys
By blood and by memory
Flooded roads, slippery leaves
and a bendy sapling tree
That appeared in the dark
when we needed it

"Lucky, little Eke,
We were lucky"

* * *

SHARED WATER

Innate as blood
The water in me
In my sweat, my tears
It runs through you too

Although they abandoned you
At two years old
Left you in a stone-cold orphanage
Gave away a piece of your soul
I know the water
That runs through your veins
Ran in their veins too

When I was tiny
You showed me patiently
How to drink from a stream
Cup my hands just so
To catch the sweet water
And let the rest of it go

Remembering
Mountain rivers in spring
Hikes to holy wells in summer
Mist and ice on the roads in winter
Waterfalls in the valley of my birth
The rain that encompassed it all

Just like blood
These sweet waters
Whether from the cup of a bright well
Or a cloud of weighted sorrow
From moorland stream or raging flood
Just like blood,
They run through the both of us
And I, your pagan daughter

Even now
The pull of the sea
She sings to you
Haunts you like a long-lost lover
In later years
Your beloved River
The dirty life-blood of London
Will eventually take you back to Her

The River
Whose water you pour
From the tap when I visit
An age-old ritual
With you ever reminding me
To let the glass sit
Allow the chlorine to evaporate
Before drinking

* * *

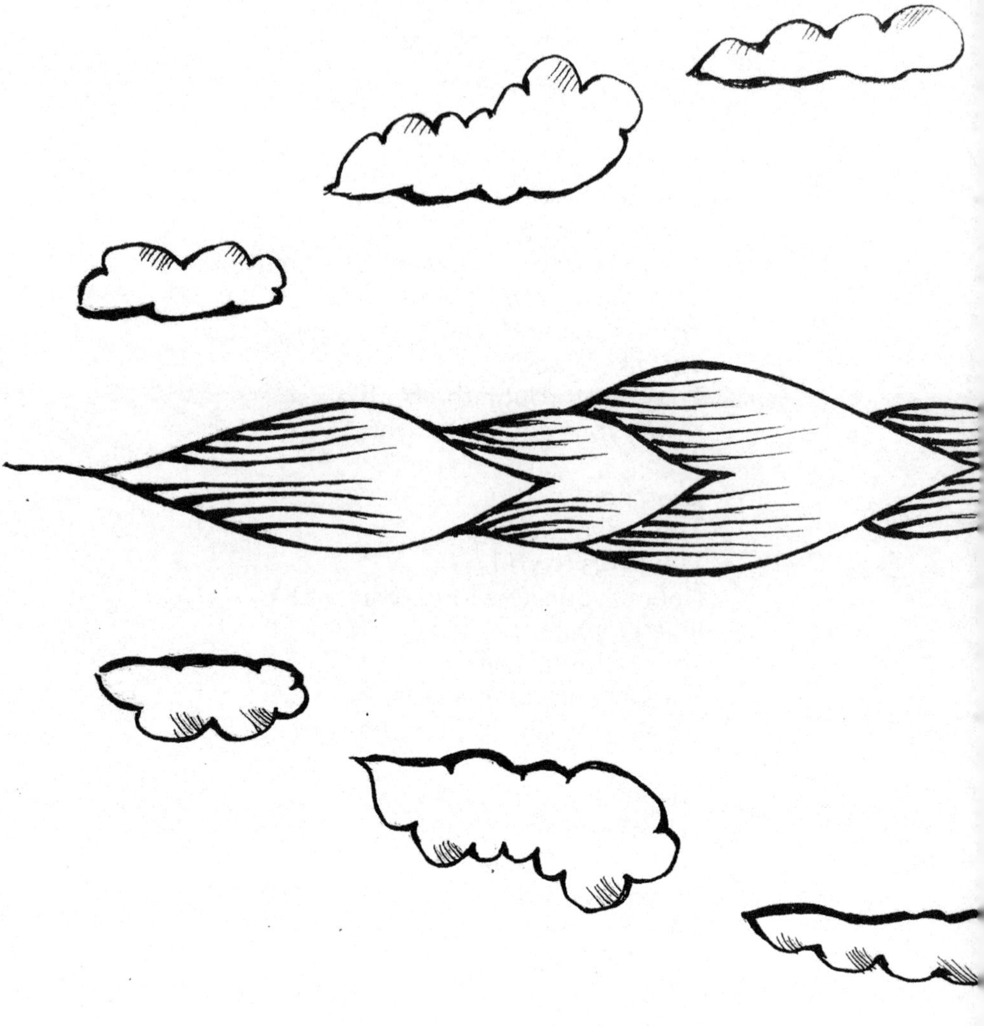

MIRROR TO THE SKY

The night
lifts its heavy skirts
To let the light
come creeping back

The mercury sea
at dawn
Like a still mirror
to the sky

With no divide
No separation
in their sleeping majesty

* * *

MOTHERLINE

Who am I without my motherline?
Without blood, bone or kin

I am the sleeping cairn in winter
The holy well in spring
Ripe with offering

I am the song in the hazel groves
Primal goddess
Carved into curves
Of the half-wild landscape

Currents of vast oceans
Playing dolphins into shore
I am the fire on the tor
Beacon of hope in the darkness

I am the stars
In my lovers' eyes
Salmon in the river
Leaping for freedom

Wolf-howl longing
In the heart of every man
Reaching for meaning

I am the thrill of focussed will
Keen edge of truth
Bright sword wielded
In service to the heart

I am the thirst for deep knowing
One who dives for pearls
In the dark waters
Of her own ocean

I am the joy of dancers on the hill
Weaving tales of stars and fire
Augmented
With the slow music of time

This is my homecoming
In these bright sparks
My hearth-song,
My belonging, my true motherline

* * *

NO CORNERS

With eyes blue-grey as the sea
There are no corners
Only curves
Between her and me

They say you choose
Your family
We chose each other
When we needed a sister
In the wilds of India
At the age of thirteen

A mirror
In whom
We could
See ourselves

No matter the years
The reflection still holds
Like a homecoming

Beyond the shimmering glass
And the wheel of time

Showing the essence
Of our sameness
Our differences
From the inside

With eyes blue-grey as the sea
There are no corners
Only curves
Between her and me

* * *

LIONHEARTED

Lionhearted kin
The courage of children
Raising each other
A community long since scattered

Reflecting it back
In memory and song
Standing in witness
To all that was done

Radiant mirrors
Sending shooting stars
From one to another

Tender light beams linking us
Like a network of human satellites
All across the globe

* * *

CRACKED OPEN

Cracked
Like a caterpillar's chrysalis

Butterfly emerging
Unfurling
Wing-damp

Into the bright unknown

* * *

APPLE MAGIC

As I drive
I eat the apples
From last autumn
Spitting seeds
Into the wind

When I'm done
I suck the core
One hand upon the wheel
The other sticky
With last year's juices

And throw it from my
Moving window
Into woven hedges
Of hazel, thorn
Briar, oak and ash

Singing grow apples
Grow again
Bring us fruit and
Sow seed again
In these wild Isles of my birth

* * *

SPRING EVENING

Sun
burning a hole
through the woods on the hill

Rooks
in the treetops

Blue skies
fading quietly
through gold into dusk

Captured
in my kitchen window;
a luminous spring evening

* * *

Blossoming, Love, Summer

GARLIC

I keep garlic
at my window
To prevent you
from entering

But in truth
I want you
To wake me
from sleeping
In the darkness
of a velvet dream

With your lips at my throat
My hot heart racing
Begging me
to invite you in

* * *

ROSES

The blossoms
On the whitethorn trees are gone
I mourn for spring

But there are roses in the hedgerows
Garden escapees
In gold, pink and scarlet hues
Weaving their thorny way
Through fern, briar
and meadowsweet

With ox-eye daisies
Dancing in attendance
Redheaded poppies
Nodding in sun-kissed fields

Bright slashes of colour
Bursting from every border
Every ditch playing host
To a troupe of travelling players
Foxgloves, flowering thyme
Bee-orchids, gentians and forget-me-nots

I might have missed
The whitethorn
But everywhere I go
There are roses growing wild
In the hedgerows
The summer is in full bloom

* * *

MEETING BY THE LAKE

After many moons of solitude
His dreams bid him
Return to the lake

Where before all was
Darkness
Reeds
Cold shadows

Now in place of his reflection
Her face shone back at him
Smiling
Delighted at his surprise
Making ripples in the water

He marvelled at her differences
Where he was dark as thunder clouds
She was golden fair
With moonlit skin

Where his eyes were deep blue storms
Filled with turbulence
Hers were slanted like a cat's
Bright cut jewels in the sun
That flashed when she laughed
She laughed a lot
As he would come to see

While he was busy
Wondering
Were reflections
Meant to be exact mirrors?
For how would it work if they were not?

She was busy
Seeing through his world-wise ways
Sizing up his innocence
Well-hidden
His tender heart
Well-bruised
And loving him all the more for it

* * *

GOOD THINGS

Bird song floating in the window
Soft down feathers of my pillow
Holding me
Sweetly
Drifting
On wisps of cloud
Between this world and the next

* * *

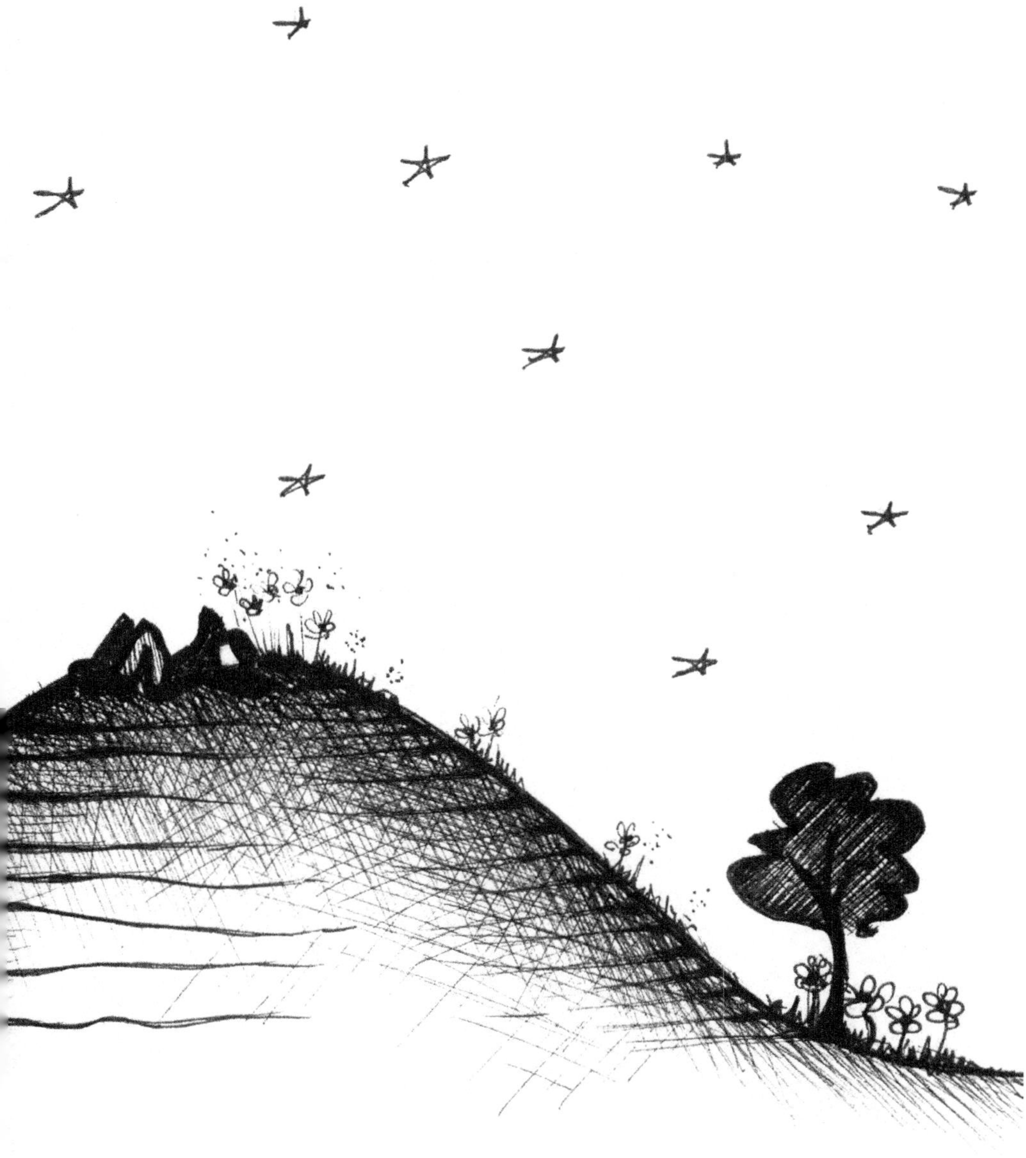

I LOVE THIS PLACE

Especially
As the sky stretches
Wide and blue above me
Empty of clouds
Sun lighting up the world
Of stone, trees and bright green fields

Especially
As the early morning light
Sets gentle fire
To the inlet outside my window
In watercolour hues
Of apricot, hot pink and wild violet

Lighting up fields
Dotted with white houses
Like a glowing disco dance floor
Making my heart shout
GOOD MORNING
To all the sleeping folks within

Especially
As last night's full moon
Hangs high above the limestone hills
In soft golden glory
Still floating in the sunrise sky

A single lantern
To remind me
Of the party I had last night
With the constellations and the stars
Oh what a night it was

* * *

IMAGINE

I am lying in a room of glass
With sunlight pouring in

Imagining
Poppies, thistles and lucifer lilies
Winking in a bright hoard of colour
At my feet

Beyond the wall
A field of golden wheat
Rippling slightly
In the wind

Imagining
A flock of pigeons
Fluttering low
Over the nodding rows
Stealing seeds
To feed their young
And fatten their plump bellies

Imagining
Wandering
Through distant golden fields
As birds swoop and flutter

Whilst above me
Broiling clouds
Of cushioned grey

Part to show again
The dazzling blues
Of their true nature

* * *

ALCHEMY

Quiet now
I make my mark
Settling to the page
With pen and ink

The story flows
In line and colour
I don't stop to think
About what goes where

Preferring trust
Over logic
However surreal
I melt into the mark-making

Letting the lines flow
Looking forward
To the reveal
At the end

When it's done
I'm just as surprised
As anyone
By the unexpected twist in the tale

The wild notes in the margins
Sketches in the corners
And scorch marks
On the canvas

✶ ✶ ✶

WHEEL OF FORTUNE

The wheel spins
through shadow
and sunlight

Through life
and death
through day and night

All the while
the Lady sings

She holds us
in her arms
with great compassion

As with practised hands
she rolls the dice

* * *

LIGHT WITHIN

There is a light within you
That burns
In the darkness
Of your own being
An inner galaxy
Perhaps
Too faint for human eyes to see

But the eyes of the soul
Have superhuman powers
A natural ability
To see the falling stars
That burn within us
Brilliant against the black

They catch the dazzling light
Of all we hold inside
The shimmer of the gold we hide
In darkened pockets
Of ourselves

When we take a chance
To look upon another
With inner sight
Long black curtains pull aside

We see each other
Like glowing lanterns
Shining two ways
Illuminating hidden pathways
Soul to soul

* * *

BEAR

There's an angry bear
With a wounded paw
Loose in the woods tonight

He is a little scary
But all I want to do is
Untangle his burrs and
Bring him honey for healing

You know
I'd wrap my arms about his neck
Brush his coat till it glowed
Make him laugh all night
If he'd let me

I can find my way
Down the woodland paths
With just a torch
And a big pot of honey

But tracking this bear
Through the pitch dark trees
With him all sore and angry
Might not be my best idea
Given our fiery history

* * *

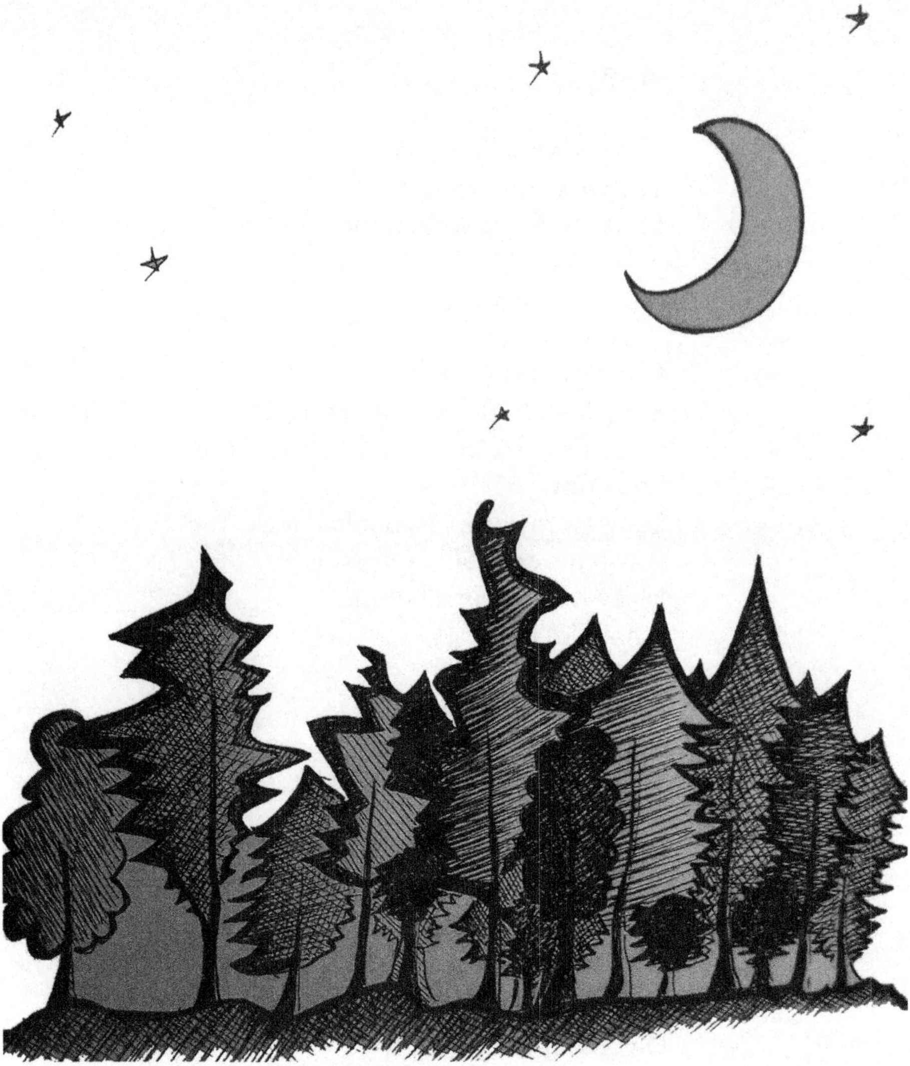

MIDSUMMER'S NIGHT

On Midsummer's night
Your window
Shaped like a sail
Of burning glass

Shone with the sun
Setting over the lake
Like a painting

In the distance
A fire on a small hill
Burnt away
All that went before

Leaving
A bright bed of embers
Caught by the camera

Reflected
In the dark pools
Of our eyes

* * *

REMEMBERED KISSES

Remembered kisses
Fingertips brushing skin
Warm breath tickling
Quiet laughter shared
With lowered lashes
In lingering moments
Just for two

* * *

FULL CIRCLE

In curls and sweeping curves
I circle back
To that small cottage on the hill
Surrounded by a grove of trees
The place where I used to live
With the girl I used to be

Dreamlike I tumble
Up the winding path of memory
Past hedges
Of oak, briar and meadowsweet
Through the orchard
Carpeted white
With fallen apple blossom
That swirls in tiny clouds
Behind me as I pass

Through the labyrinthine herb garden
With its spiralling paths
Sunk into the hill
Framed in warm stone

Sunkissed
I run bare-footed
Fast across fresh-cut grass
On the small round lawn
Through the arch
Up the crescent steps
To the front door

Everything curved
Stone, branch, wall, path
Everything turning full circle
As I run back
Through the years
Through the door
And take her hands in mine

Now two sets of mirrored eyes
Reflecting cobalt skies
Study each other like a puzzle

"Always remember
You are made of sunshine"

She laughs and pulls away
Bright with summer love and freckles
Breaking the spell

"Sure, how could I forget?
It's in my very bones"

But I know, I know
There's inclement weather to come
Oh, how I long to protect her
To step back through time
Wrap her in a cloak of starlight
Bring her home again
Full circle

* * *

UNTIL ALWAYS

I cannot tell you why
The wind blows me
Back down this valley
To the bones of the mountain
We built on salt flats

Why the scents of apple blossom
Meadowsweet, sea-spray
And pine-scented bonfires
Remind me so of you

I cannot say exactly why
I wander in the shadow of tall pines
Beside rushing rivers
Forded only by log rafts
Or crossed on hay-scented horseback

I cannot voice the longing inside me
For petrol blue skies
For hurricanes in the hay fields
For young love's kiss
For the golden glory of summers past
In all their laughing mayhem

I will not name
The things I miss
Nor write another lengthy list
Of all the places
We've kissed and loved
And lost to folly
However special they may be

I will not speak
The secrets we share
The scars of the fierce, bright love
We both still bear

But in the quiet dark
Of sleepless nights
I do long for us to lay down arms
To take off our armour piece by piece
And touch again the beating hearts
That lie beneath
These tender skins

In restless dawns
I wake alone
To a distant symphony of crows
Beyond the blinds

I long to turn through time and whisper
"There is a field I'll meet you there"
The things we've said and done do not matter
I will love you until always
But I cannot find the words
In this cacophony

In the teeming silence
That surrounds us now
I am hoping you can still hear
My living heartbeat

When you stop to listen,
Feel my resonant love reflected
In the wild poetry
Of this quiet land

For whatever else has changed
Here, our love song will remain
Until always

* * *

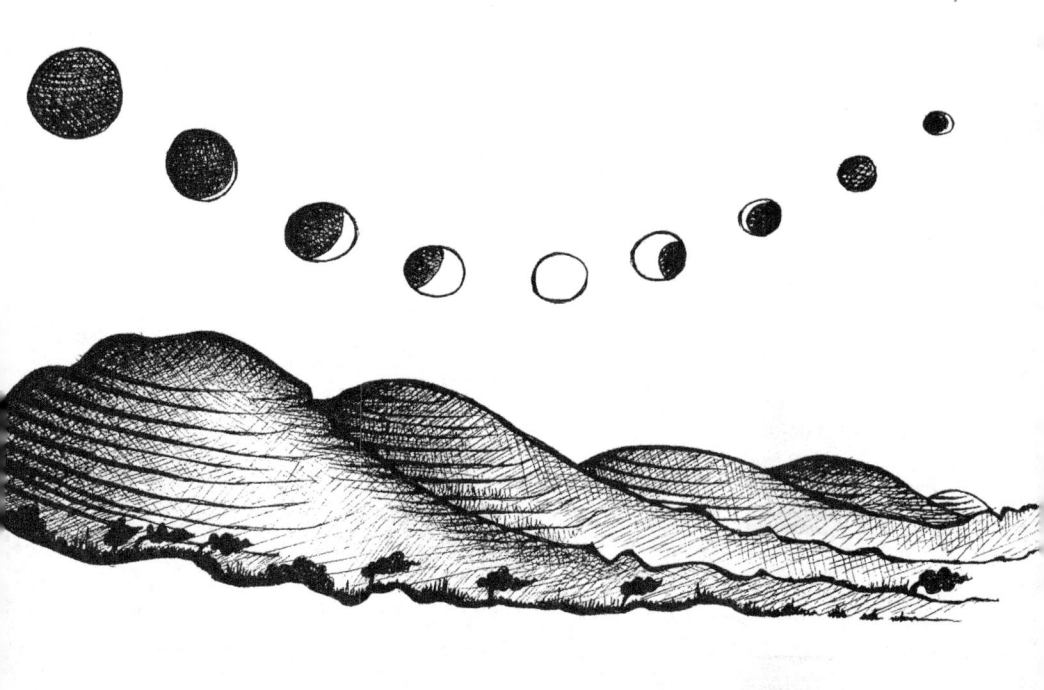

Change, Loss, Death, Autumn

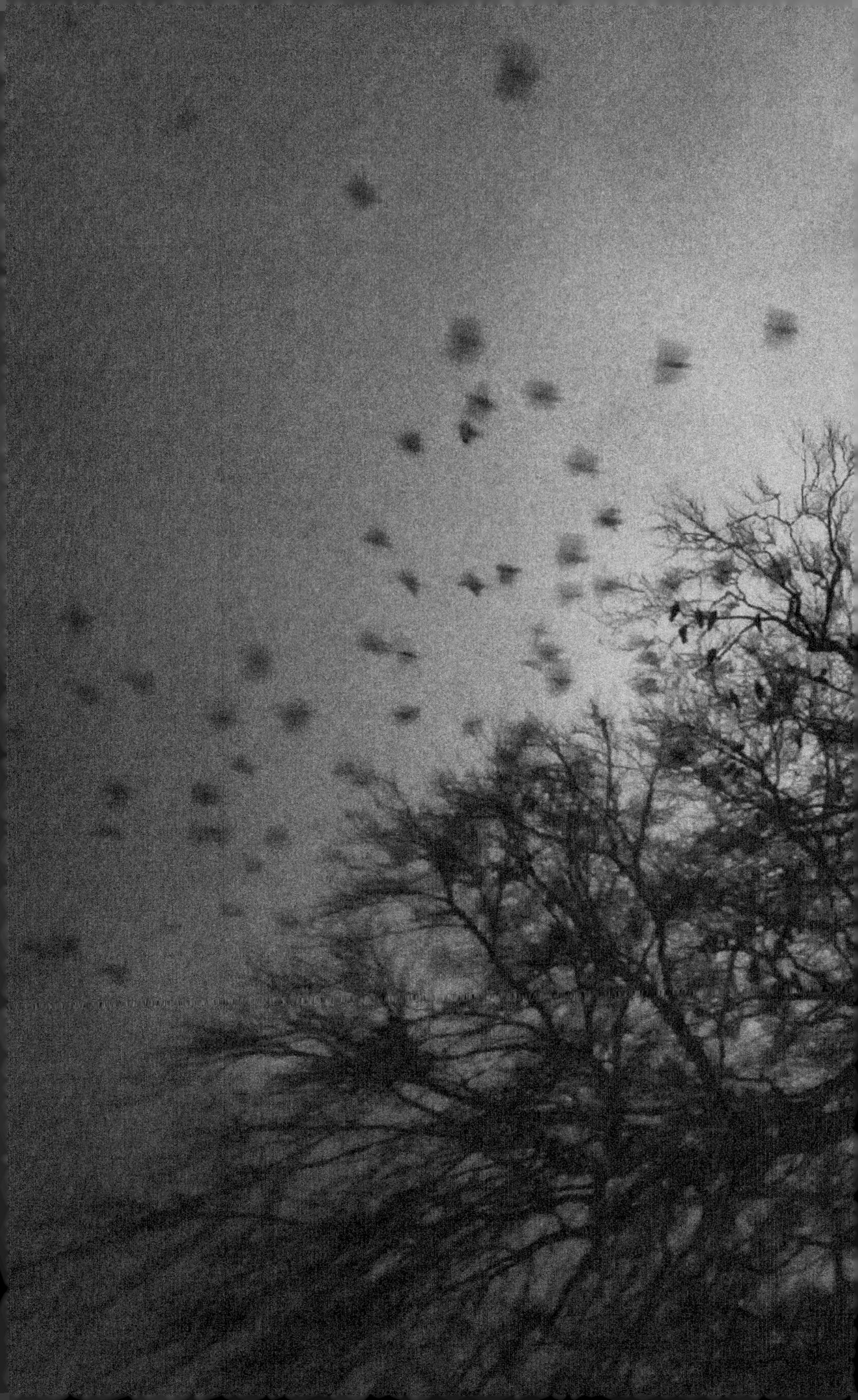

TWILIGHT

A cloud of rooks
Across the brooding sky
Do fly and swoop and caw
As night considers falling

Almost,
But not quite yet
Does darkness rise
To frame the quietening town

For now we sit and marvel
At the slowly falling twilight

The cloud of wheeling rooks
All singing in the fading day
Above the stand of pines
Beside the river

Before they go to roost
This autumn night

* * *

LONE WOLF

The wolf in me
Calls to the wolf in you
Echoes
'Cross valleys
Of a thousand neolithic dawns
We sang together

Heartbeat
Calling through the void
From my mountain top to yours
In pine-scented
Steep-sloped glory

Rough-hewn rock face
Carpeted in bright berries
Free roaming prairie
Rich with wilderness
Herb-scented
Star-strung
With room to run
Below the singing moon

Lone wolf ranges
Through a solitary paradise
Free as an eagle
In untouched skies
King of the hills
Master of the hunt
Lover of the wild

He prowls
Silhouetted mountains
In sovereign light
Singing freedom's song
He bows to none

But on quiet nights
His heart
Still howls
For more

* * *

HELD HOSTAGE

Their yesteryear goes unnamed
Like a large wooden box in the hall
They walk around
It remains locked,
Without labels
Containing memories
It's easier to bury

If they only dared
Lift the lid together
They may just find
A doorway to another world
A dragon's hoard of treasure

Hidden in shadow
Unrecognised

Instead
Held hostage by time
They talk about the weather

If they could
Bare their souls again
Find the courage to navigate
Past sleeping dragons and old mistakes
The key to the enchanted door
Lies waiting in the box

But for now
He'll stand and clear the table
Don his cap
With an awkward smile
That doesn't match
The lingering look in his eyes

"Thanks for dinner"
"No problem, call in anytime"

When the front door closes
She'll wash the plates
Put on the kettle
While the radio's playing
'Because the Night'
Then 'Wuthering Heights'
Drawing her back to times gone by
The wooden box remains unopened

* * *

A HEADY INTIMACY

Feather-light
Your touch upon my skin
Reminds me
Of so much
I had forgotten

A passing breath of air
Brings me the warm,
Woody scent of you
Overlaid with lemon soap

The tickle of an eyelash
A momentary flutter upon my cheek
As we both pause
Between in-breath and out

A heady intimacy
Rearing its head between us
For a heartbeat
Achingly familiar
But long since passed

The moment breaks
As we each turn away
To smile our hellos
Towards another
Cheeks flushed

Avoiding eye contact
In the busy hallway
Filled with welcome chatter
And discarded raincoats

* * *

WASH ME CLEAN

Tonight I bathe in shadows
As the late rains
Come pouring down
On the glazed roof above me

Sudden tears flowing
Percussive drops
Drumming insistently
Upon my heart

A flood on the glass
I lie beneath
Breathing slowly
Watching rivulets
Running quietly

Listening to the downpour
From the darkening couch
In my wee conservatory
Rivers of rain
Washing me clean

* * *

DEMETER

Come Autumn
Her daughter
Begins her descent
Down through
Seven gates to
Reclaim her crown

Come Winter
The Goddess
Dreams of the dead
But the gates to Hades
Will not open
Far below
The dark queen reigns
Beside her consort king

At the season's turn
The Goddess mourns
With golden tears
For the realm of the dead
Will not surrender
Her dark daughter
Again until Spring

* * *

ASHES OF THE MORNING

I burned with them last evening
As the light left the sky
Birds in the trees
Quietened to sleep
In the canopies

I witnessed flames burning
In the hearts
Of my foremothers
My grandmothers
All the way back to Eve

I burned
With my mother's paintings
Image of line and lineage
Interwoven
With blood red thread

Memories and dreams
Of those
Who went before me
Collected and
Written in her hand

It was a mighty fire
Fierce and bright with life
Hungry for the canvas
Yet later quiet
In the darkness
Of the last embers' glow

Now in the ashes of the morning
As the birds take up their songs
Fire smoking, images gone
I am the one left living
The last of my line
Whose heart still burns
For love, truth and freedom

* * *

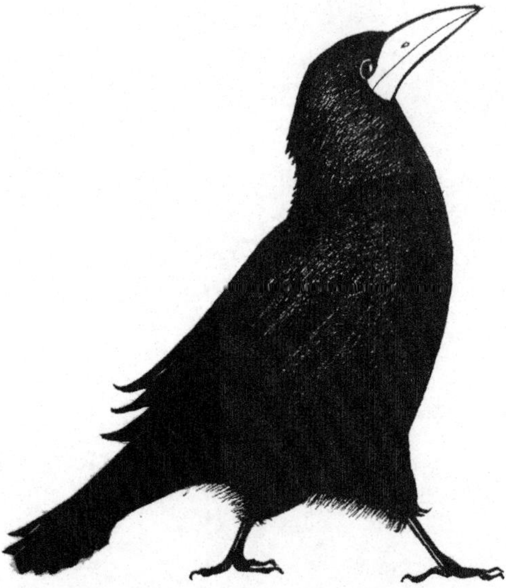

TRICKSTER

Oh sister crow
Clever corvid
Beady-eyed
Flying low

Shape-shifter
Shadow-hand
Wisdom-holder
Battle-seeker

Death-messenger
Portal-keeper
Story-hoarder
Eyeball-eater

Oh trickster
Sister crow
Clever corvid
You might know

Where have all the Ravens gone?
Does the Morrigan live on
In your shadow?

* * *

WHEN DEATH COMES CALLING

On Halloween
My father died
I have been busy
Arranging his funeral
Painting his coffin
In a collage
Of boats and starry skies

But when Death comes calling
She does the rounds
For on the shining isle
My beautiful wolf
Left without a goodbye

And I
Stone-weighted
Lead-heavy
Heart-shattered
To lose two best friends
In a swooping moment
Of ravens' wings

Through clouds of tears
This evening
A vision came
The two of them walking together
Under boughs of emerald
In a deep forest glade

Pine-scented
Light-motes dancing
Through mossy evergreens
Buoyant with the joy
Of wild places
With no more fear
Of the beckoning night

Is it so
I wonder
That everyone we love
Who has gone before us
Is out there together
Gambolling
Through the universe
Surrounded by light?

* * *

JOURNEY

He has begun his journey
Into the darklands

Where he will take
the Reaper's hand
When his time is done

He will step
into his boat
Set the sails
and sail away

It will be
just himself and the sea
All the way
to the bright shores
Of his new beginning

All the while
We on his old shore
Will be here singing

* * *

SANCTUARY

I take sanctuary
In my cozy corner
My familiar nook

On my dark green velvet couch
In its storm-grey-blanket softness
Curled in a hot-water-bottle bear hug
In my cushion-piled haven
Where I am safe
Against soaring night skies

While twilight patrols
Swoop and caw
In black-winged flutters
At my attic window
Waves crash
On silhouetted rocks below
I know I will come to no harm
in my sky-harbour of blankets

Here my tender heart
Is fiercely held
In shelter
Cocooned
From storm-blown seas
Wrapped for a time in velvet
I am safe; I am safe

My mountain eyrie
Woven in cloud
Hidden from eagle eyes;
A place of true sanctuary

* * *

SLOW LIGHT

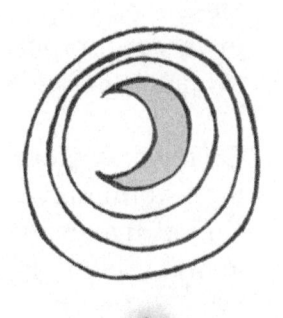

Awake in the predawn
Dim blue light
Slow-reaching
Across rooftops

The crows are not yet
In conversation

In this slow light
I have not unfurled
From below my warm duvet
To greet the day

I will soon, I promise
But not quite yet

* * *

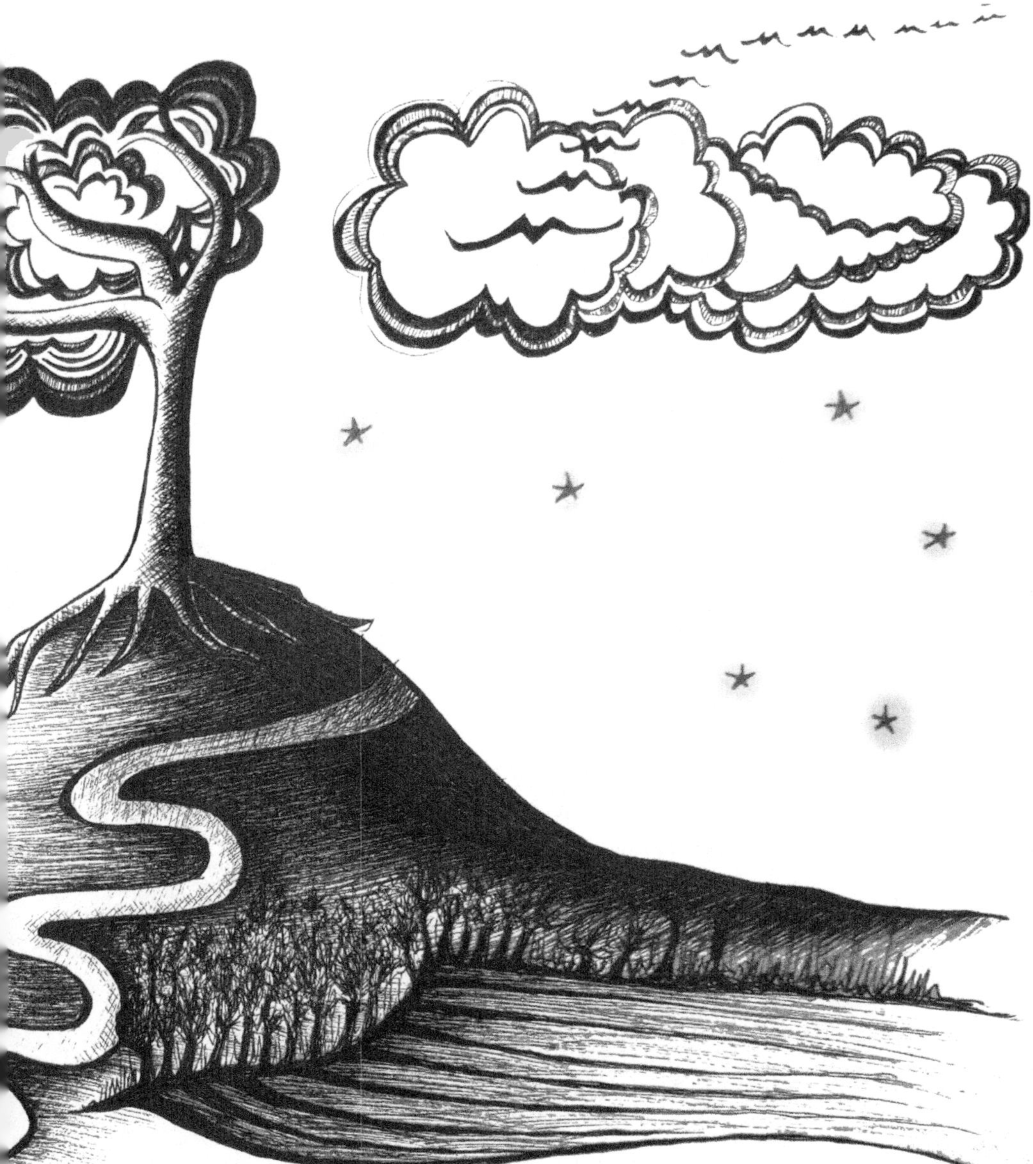

WATCHING THE WORLD FROM MY WINDOW

Watching the leaves
Fall and tumble
From the trees

Now the wind picks them up
In its tricksy fingers
Dances down the lane
Laughing and
Dropping them
Everywhere

She spins and swirls away from me
Leaping the hedge
Of thorn and hazel
Interwoven with brambles
Scattered with ivy
Disappearing into the cow-field
At the foot of the hill
In a sudden whirl of colour

Watching the world from my window
Low light on the water
Momentary fire in the trees
Herbs gone to seed in pots
Fading thistles in the garden
The last of the berries
In the hedges withering

Autumn is upon us
The season of letting go
Has come round again
Cattle in the hills
Birds wheeling overhead

I can hear the call from the mountains
That frame my quiet days
In voices of dark stone
Singing all change
All change

* * *

IN THE CITY OF SAND

The time may come in the City of Sand
When you take down the walls you have built
Block by sandstone block
You may awaken one day
Decide to remove the barricades
Of oaken pallet, rubble and spear

Tired of the siege,
You may take down the stacks of rusting tin
That keep the monsters from getting in
Dismantle the tunnels
Lined with old teddy-bears
Wired to blow when compromised
Fences built with black-eyed fear

You may begin to clear away
Brightly painted wooden carts,
Piles of broken fishing pots
Bicycle wheels with no spokes
Take the outer banks apart
Raise the rusting portcullis
Step out to greet the day

At last you may surrender the battlements
You have walked for so long
Protecting your songs
With the ferocity of a mother tiger's love

You have done well, my friend
Building a city
From the sand of broken dreams
Holding it against all odds
And all imagined enemies
But this world cannot hurt you

Stand down the vats of burning oil
If you will
Open the city gates
Let the songs of freedom roll on in
This is your awakening

When the caravan of colour
Makes its way through barren plains
Bringing hope, flow and laughter in its baskets
Welcome the day with open arms
When you are lonely in the City of Sand
It is time to remember again
The magician that you are

You can make fire with your hands
Travel on the wind to distant lands
You can create new worlds
With simple words
If you'll only let them go
To find their wings
Just as they are written
In the cloudless ink of new beginnings

Retire your trusty soldiers of tin
Let the flying circus in
You may at last dance free
Beyond the city walls
You spent so long building

This has always been so
Now it's time to remember
Find the dragon's hoard of jewels
You have carefully hidden
For safekeeping
Deep in the mountains of your soul

* * *

Wisdom, Grace, Renewal, Winter

THRESHOLD

Here,
Where wind is sharp
Light is fresh
And earth still sings
In a cascade of faded glory
The door to winter is opening

Come
To the threshold with me
Step through
I will bring you
To the place
Where new beginnings
Begin

* * *

A STORM WITH NO NAME

The wind whistles and
Howls in the chimney

The bins outside are getting
Roughed up in the blow
Thrown against the low stone wall
Small wheels spinning
Lids blown open

Sure it's just a wintery gale
A storm with no name
Come in from the sea

Whipping up trouble
On a darkened night
Whirling last summer's leaves
Around the house
As it rattles and sings in the eaves

Curled up in a small stone cottage
On a dark lane
With just the fire for company
An ordinary winter's night in

Oh the Wild West coast
Was ne'er so aptly named

* * *

SANCTA MARIA

Tears fall upon holy ground
As I light a line of candles
In Mary's chapel

I pray to the goddess of the skies
To light my way
Through the dark nights
Before me

* * *

STRIPPED AWAY

In the aftermath of the storm
where trees and rocks have fallen
Cleared by a tempest of tears

Tumbling debris torn down
washed clean by the rain
Stolen by the waves
of the dancing sea

Layers of the earth;
my life exposed
Lines of colour
in a raw seam of clay

From a distance
just stripes in the cliff face
All pretence stripped away

* * *

FIRST FROST

The earth has frozen overnight
Frost-tipped grass crackling underfoot
I walk out to greet the sinking moon
Whose yellow globe is falling
Through the lowest branches
Of the ash tree beside my house

For long moments she is cradled
In its black and leafless arms
Silhouetted against the dark indigo sky

Then she sinks in slow motion
Into the vast arms of the sleeping planet
Until all that remains
Is a glowing hum of warm gold
Painted in a thin line of beauty
Across the horizon
Like an afterthought

I am left standing
On the cold, old ground
Feet like ice-blocks with pin-pricks in them
Robe wrapped close about my shivering body
Hugging myself for warmth

I watch the stars fade and the sky lighten
Imagining again the moon's descent
Down below the ocean
And further, into the deep heart of the earth
Far below the first frost of winter

* * *

OLD SPELLS

Frozen in the city
I found a black witch's coat
In a charity shop

I wove a half-remembered spell
Into the fine woollen fabric
To keep me from the cold

And pulled the wide pointy hood
Down low upon my ears
To brave the early winter chills
Of the Wild Heath Road

To my surprise I found
That only my fingers were icy
While the rest of me
Bathed in the warmth
Of the witch-coat-glow

So now you see
Those old half-spells and weaving songs
Taught to you by your granny
Beside the sleepy fire
On winter's nights
Of long-ago

Work so much better
Than you know

* * *

WINTER QUEEN

The Winter Queen
Raises her mantle
An evergreen canopy

As we feast and toast
The dying year
In shelter and sanctuary

With a hundred burning candles
We praise her
This deep midwinter's night

* * *

THE LONGEST NIGHT

After this
The longest night
Where light creeps back
Into places of shadow

In the darkness of
The deepest well
At the dip of the year
When all stands still
For a moment

In the silence of winter
In the place between breaths
Where endings and beginnings meet

After a heartbeat
When the dark veil lifts
Dawn burns bright away the mist

Yes
After this
The longest night
After the vigil
After the fight

Where we can claim
Every shade
Of light and truth

Here, I will know myself
Again
Anew

* * *

GRACE

A moment descending
A breath that eases and opens
Out through the kitchen window
Past the hard lines
Of the library roof
Into the beyond

The long sky at sunset
Rooks calling
Across the indigo hues
Of a curled-in dusk

True colours of the gentle heart
Opening
Stretching
Streaking the deep blue horizon
With its tender, vibrant love

Golden touch
A glimmer of light
Here for this moment only
Held briefly
In cupped hands
Present in all things
If we let it be

* * *

THE CAILLEACH TREE

Her twisted branches arch
from root to tip
on the barren hillside

In solitary silhouette;
a dancer's joy

Earth hugging
Wind burnt
Sky sung

Light streaming
through her eloquent fingers;
She is the Cailleach tree

* * *

QUIVER SHOT

Walking the river
In the late winter sun
Coffee in hand
I breathe in the bright air

Frost-tipped
Scented with mossy richness
Filling the cracks
In my heart with gold
One by one

Peace beckons
In a red robin's flutter
Twitter of finches
In the changing light
Lure of unlit fires
Calling me to distant fields

A heron sits
Watching the water
Reminding me
Of all the beauty
I cannot see

Now a duck drifts past
In a quiet arrow-rake of ripples
Another following, and another
Like a quiver shot in slow motion
Opening me to the day

Steady rhythm of feathers
Gliding through air and water
Straight to the centre
A shot to the heart
Guiding me home

* * *

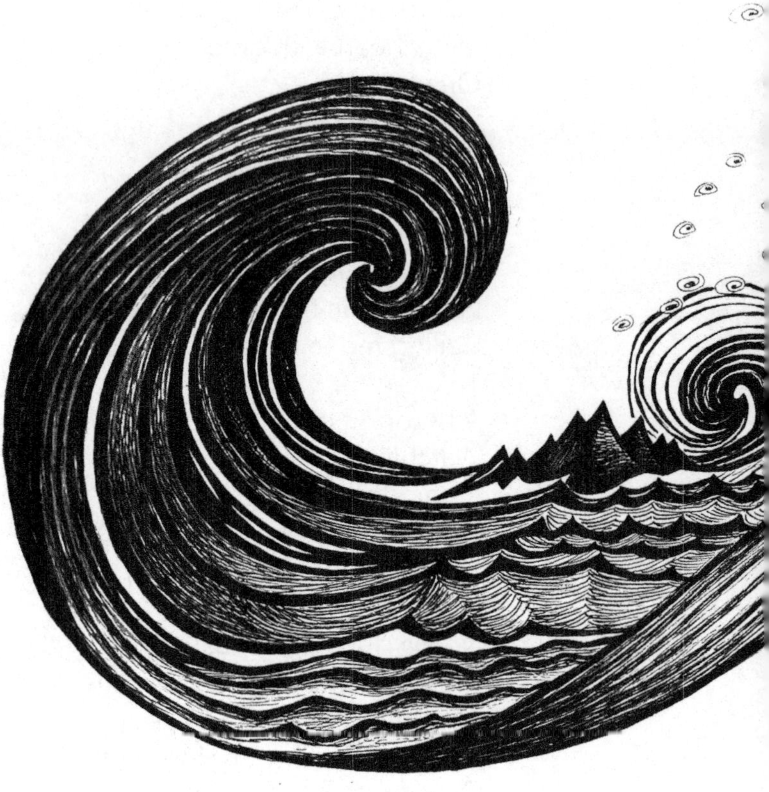

SEA SPRAY

In this vast ocean
Of consciousness
I realise

We are but droplets
Floating
Through space and time

Like sea spray
On wild Atlantic shores
In wintertime

* * *

HOPE KINDLES HOPE

Hope kindles
like a spark
amongst leaves
in a dark forest

Songbirds
silent and sleeping
are wing-tucked
in the dank mist
Nothing can rouse them

Until
Small glowing
shards of sunshine
pierce the murk
like golden arrows
shot to ground

Through branches, briars
and fern-choked glades
Twigs wrapped in moss
repel their advances

But in the glow
of quiet beams
Wings unfurl
Feathers stretch
Gilded throats
begin to sing

Tentative at first
then brightening
Scattering notes
like sparks
in the dark forest

Hope kindling
Hope kindling hope
For spring is come at last

* * *

Epilogue

UNMAPPED TERRITORY

There is a flicker in me
A spark
That whispers
Of new beginnings
Though it's hard to see
When I look at it directly

But soften my gaze
And I can feel
The sizzle of heat
That dances like fireflies
At the edge of my vision

Beckoning me onwards
Across untrodden moors
Bidding me trust and step
Through the sea of heather
That runs out past the city
Further than I can see
Into unmapped territory

* * *

BRIGHT HORIZON

I have been heavy
Leaden
Like a hot-air balloon
Ballast-strung
Task-tied

Straining at my tethers
Struggling to carry
The solid weight
Of the vast earth behind me
In my incessant bid for freedom

Now comes the heady rush
The calculated dash
With all tethers cut
Ballast
Thrown from my basket
At great height

Soaring
Sky-bound
Giddy
With the sudden
Sense of lightness

Setting sail again
On currents of air
High above the clouds
I set my course for Spring

Face kissed with freckles
Hair tossed to the wind

Eyes narrow
Glinting fierce

Into the wild glare
Of the bright horizon

* * *

P.S.

If this is my postscript
Then let it be sweet
As berries
Ripe
On sun-kissed hillsides

Hearts like kites
Flying as we run
Barefooted
With juice-stained lips

Freckled noses
Laughing at clouds
Rolling soft
Through changing skies

Like a vast bed
Of downy comfort
Pillowed in blue
With sunsets a-plenty
In breath-taking hues

I would not ask
The weather be perfect
Nor the people only good
Nor the days only rosy

But that we are shown
Skies filled with beauty
Hearts filled with treasure
Days of quiet pleasure

Always reminded
Wherever we look
Whatever we see
To open bright eyes;

Cast your sight wide
For life is rich
With magnificent views

* * *

NOTES

Innocence, Childhood, Spring

CHANGELING CHILD
In Irish, Welsh and Scottish folklore, a 'changeling' is a faerie child, left by the 'good people' in place of a stolen human child, to grow up in its stead. In older times, people often believed that a sickly child was a changeling, the real child having been taken to *Tír Na nÓg* (Land of Eternal Youth; Ireland) or *Annwn* (The Otherworld; Wales) to live evermore with the faeries. It was a kindness sometimes, to believe that their real child was living forever, in a land of delight and plenty. As a child, fascinated by old faerie-tales, with no true sense of 'home,' I sometimes wondered if I was in fact a changeling.

FREEFALL
Eke (pronounced "eek") was a baby nick-name, given to me while I was still 'growing into' my big names. My father called me *Eke-Bach* or "little Eke" in Welsh.

MOTHERLINE
Written after the death of both my parents, as an exploration into personal lineage and what 'belonging' means, when I read this poem back, I realised I had accidentally written an homage to the 'Song of Amhairgin,' which is thought to be the first poem ever written in Ireland.

The stories tell us that Amhairgin (pronounced "av-er-gin") was a warrior bard and druid of the Milesians, who came to Ireland between 3500 and 1000 years BC. When the Tuatha Dé Danann threw a magical mist around the island, Amhairgin spoke a powerful incantation which parted the mists and allowed the Milesians to land. Naming himself as a reflection of all the magical places and creatures of Ireland wove Amhairgin into the fabric of its sovereignty. The 'Song of Amhairgin' was recorded in the Book of Invasions – *Lebor Gabála Érenn* – an oral history of the peoples of Ireland, which was compiled and written down in the 11th century.

Blossoming, Love, Summer

UNTIL ALWAYS
"There is a field I'll meet you there" is a line from Jalal al-Din Rumi – 13th century Persian poet. Rumi was an Islamic scholar, Sufi mystic and radical spiritual teacher. The full quote is: "Out beyond ideas of wrongdoing and right doing there is a field, I'll meet you there."

Change, Loss, Death, Autumn

HELD HOSTAGE
'Because the Night' is a song by Patti Smith — co-written with Bruce Springsteen. 'Wuthering Heights' is a song by Kate Bush, based on the 19th century novel by Emily Bronte. Both songs were written in 1977 and released as singles in 1978.

DEMETER
This poem touches on the tale of Demeter, ancient Greek goddess of the harvest, and the abduction of her daughter Persephone, by Hades, the god of the underworld. In Greek mythology, when Persephone is taken, Demeter grieves for her and casts a blight across the land. Zeus is asked to intervene, and it is agreed that to keep the balance, Persephone return to her mother for half the year (spring, summer) and spend the second half of the year (autumn, winter) with her husband, in the realm of the dead. This creates a sophisticated symbolism for the dance of the seasons, and mirrors the Celtic calendar, which descends through the gates of autumn into winter at the festival of Samhain (31st October).

I have also referenced the Sumerian myth of the goddess Inanna's descent to the underworld to meet her sister Ereshkigal, in which she has to pass seven gates, and at each one, give up the vestiges of her worldly identity, in order to eventually face her sister the Queen of the Dead, to die and be reborn anew.

TRICKSTER
In Irish mythology, the Morrigan — in her plural form as the *Morrígna* — is one of the original triple goddesses of Ireland. In her single form she is the *Mór-Ríoghain* or 'great queen,' a goddess of war, death and wild last nights. The Morrigan is a shape-changer, and in the old stories, often takes the form of crow or raven on battlefields, seen as a messenger from the Otherworld, or portent of death. In some tales she is also said to take the shape of a wolf.

Wisdom, Grace, Renewal, Winter

THE CAILLEACH TREE
Inspired by the solitary, windswept trees on the wild west coast of Ireland, which are literally sculpted by the wind into the most amazing dancing shapes. Some see them as forlorn, but I see them as a beautiful reflection of this majestic, elemental landscape.

Cailleach (pronounced "kyle-yach") is Irish for old crone or hag. In Irish, Scots and Manx mythologies, *An Cailleach* is the Winter Witch – hailed as one of the oldest sovereign Celtic goddesses. She is intrinsic to the winter months, to the mountains and wild places, known also as 'the veiled one' who guides us into the dark half of the year, through the gateway to her winter realms. There are many places named after her, including the Beara peninsula in Co. Cork, Hag's Head in Co. Clare, and *Sliabh na gCailli* in Co. Meath, where the neolithic tombs of Loughcrew are sited.

The stories also tell us that she is a powerful creatrix; her magical staff brings the great freeze, her tears of sorrow the great thaw, she is the winter wind which sculpts the land, across which she bounds, scattering rocks from her apron, creating hills and mountains in her wake.

ACKNOWLEDGEMENTS

In gratitude to my dear friends and familiars who have patiently read the tidal waves of writing I have sent them over the years.

To my writing groups, for their consistent support in creating collaborative containers in which to nurture and grow each other's words.

To the work and writings of Beth Kempton, which have provided forum and sanctuary for my writing voice through the turbulences of the last few years. Honestly, forever grateful.

To Joe Cavanaugh and Mark Terry for believing so wholeheartedly in me and my poetry, especially as an unknown writer from a distant land. For their enthusiastic embrace of this project bringing their unfailing professionalism and creativity to the table, as editor, designer and as publishers.

To my friends Caoilte and Finola for casting keen eyes over the details written *as Gaeilge*, to Doris for believing in faerie-tales, to Paudie for the wild-haired photos, and to Abha for giving me her bird's eye view.

And lastly, to Miten, for seeing the magic in my words, and for his determination to pull the vast boxes of writing out from beneath my bed and see them published; with a classically prosaic, "It's time Mallix, let me help."

With massive gratitude, love and thanks to you all.
Couldn't have done it without you.

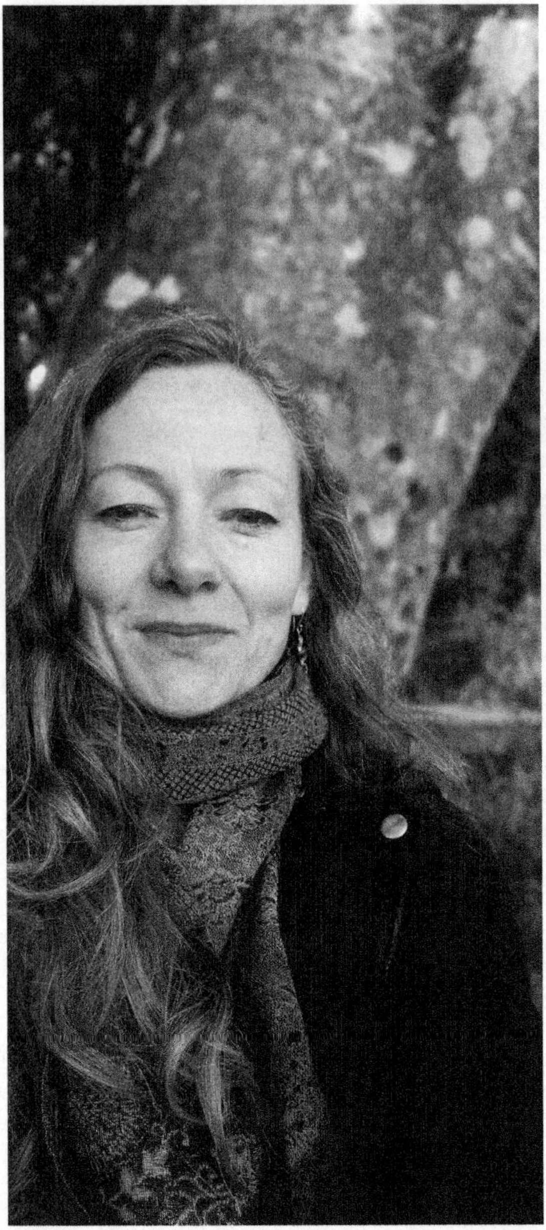

About Mallika McCarthy

Born in a Welsh mountain valley, halfway between London and the west coast of Ireland, Mallika spent her childhood zigzagging from Europe to India to Australia, with plenty of adventures in between.

Carrying a suitcase of old faerie-tales, her life a patchwork quilt of places, stitched together with bright thread; Ireland has always been one of her homes.

Having worked as singer, songwriter; fire-dancer, street performer; stage manager, theatre-tech, waitress, bookseller; administrator, voice coach and yoga teacher, Mallika has worn hats in many worlds, but writing has always been her first love.

With most of her family now dead and gone, she has come to realise that it's not where you come from that matters, but where you belong.

She has made her home in County Clare, on the stormy wild west coast, where you might find her teaching, writing, singing, yoga-ing, doodling, reading, baking; or out lighting bonfires, talking to the rooks under seasonal skies.

Inspired by ancient tales of myth and magic, Mallika has been writing ever since she could hold a stick in a sandpit, but most of what she has written lives in a proverbial box under her bed. Until now. This is her first collection of poetry.

Printed in Great Britain
by Amazon